Andrew
Happy 9th Birthday.
Love
x Gran, Grandad
x Edna John x

ANYONE CAN BE A CARTOONIST

Peter COUPE

PETER COUPE

ARCTURUS

PUBLISHED BY ARCTURUS PUBLISHING LIMITED
FOR BOOKMART LIMITED
REGISTERED NUMBER - 2372865
TRADING AS BOOKMART LIMITED
DESFORD ROAD
ENDERBY
LEICESTER
LE9 5AD

THIS EDITION PUBLISHED - 1997

ISBN. 1 900032 76 7

CONTENTS...

GO!

BACK TO BASICS...

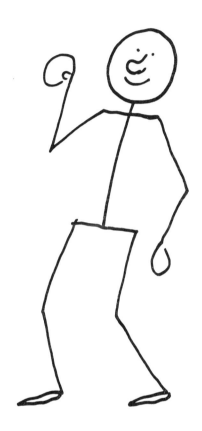

EVERYTHING YOU NEED TO KNOW TO START DRAWING CARTOONS!

MATCHSTICK FIGURES...

IT IS MUCH EASIER TO DRAW IF YOU HAVE SOME SIMPLE GUIDELINES TO FOLLOW.

A MATCHSTICK FIGURE MAKES AN IDEAL SET OF GUIDELINES FOR DRAWING A CARTOON FIGURE...

...MUCH EASIER THAN STARTING OUT WITH A BLANK SHEET OF PAPER!

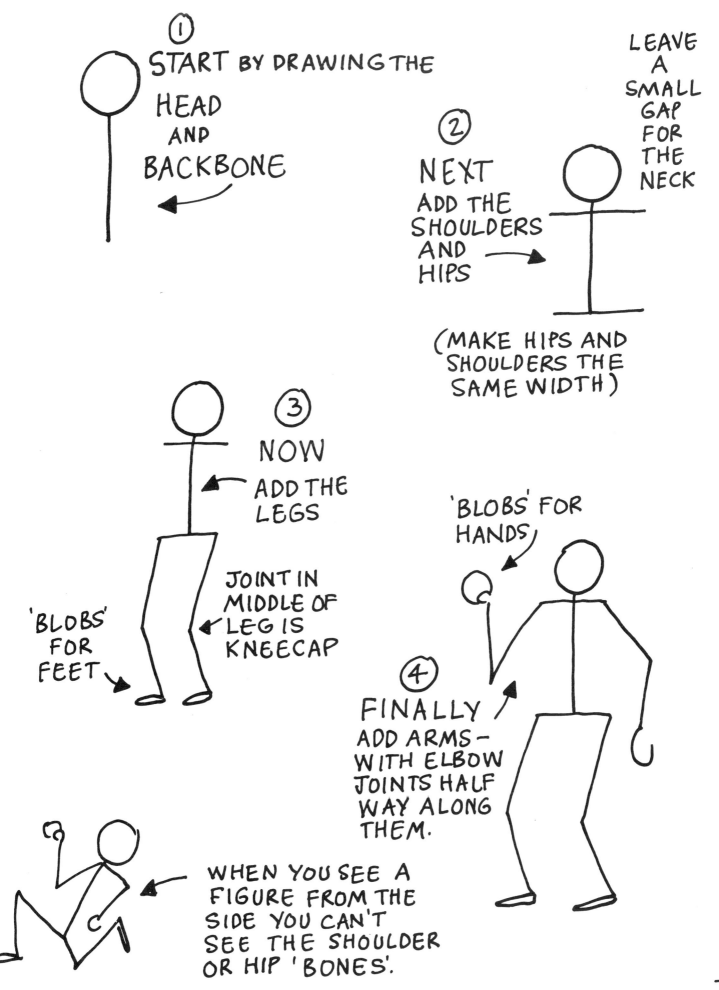

① START BY DRAWING THE HEAD AND BACKBONE

LEAVE A SMALL GAP FOR THE NECK

② NEXT ADD THE SHOULDERS AND HIPS

(MAKE HIPS AND SHOULDERS THE SAME WIDTH)

③ NOW ADD THE LEGS

JOINT IN MIDDLE OF LEG IS KNEECAP

'BLOBS' FOR FEET

'BLOBS' FOR HANDS

④ FINALLY ADD ARMS — WITH ELBOW JOINTS HALF WAY ALONG THEM.

WHEN YOU SEE A FIGURE FROM THE SIDE YOU CAN'T SEE THE SHOULDER OR HIP 'BONES'.

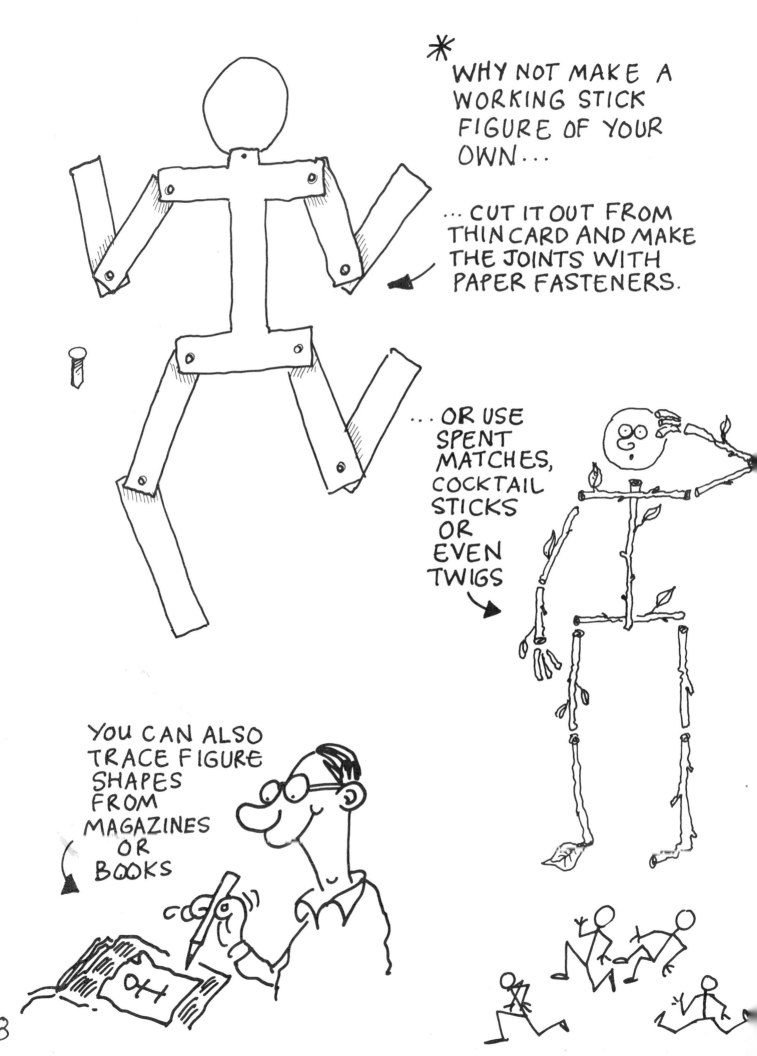

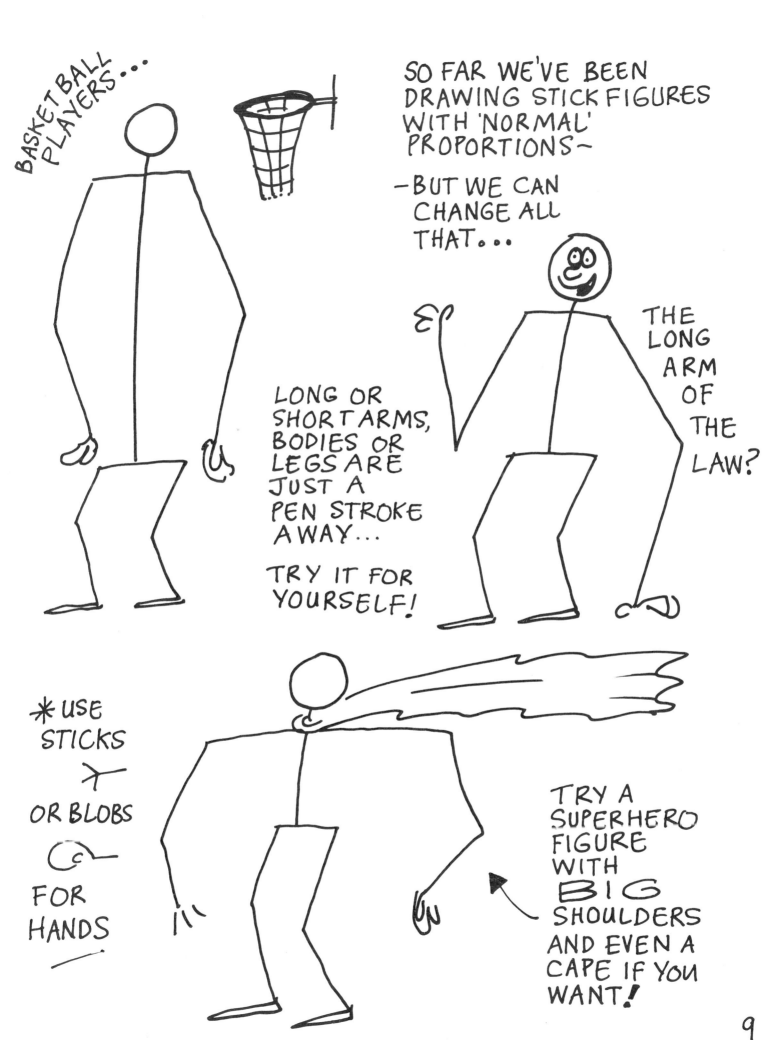

NICE SUIT-
DO YOU
HAVE IT
IN A
PIN
STRIPE?

OUR NEXT JOB IS TO ADD SOME
CLOTHES TO OUR STICK FIGURES.

START WITH SIMPLE BLOB AND
TUBE SHAPES DRAWN ROUND
THE STICKS.

DON'T WORRY ABOUT
ADDING DETAILS - KEEP
IT NICE AND SIMPLE.

◄ COLLAR

ZIG-ZAG FOR
COAT LAPEL.

◄ SIMPLE
FEET

* DRAW A STICK FIGURE
ON A PIECE OF PAPER-
THEN PUT YOUR DRAWING
PAPER OVER IT - THAT
WAY YOU
HAVE NO
PENCIL
LINES TO
RUB OUT
WHEN
YOU'VE
FINISHED
THE
DRAWING

* USE BOOKS AND
MAGAZINES FOR
FASHION IDEAS AND
INSPIRATION.

LET'S DO THIS IN EASY STEPS...

WOW...THAT'S MY KIND OF GIRL!

① START WITH YOUR SIMPLE STICK FIGURE...

② 'FATTEN' IT OUT WITH BLOBS OR SAUSAGE SHAPES...

③ SMOOTH OUT THESE SIMPLE SHAPES TO FORM CLOTHES!

REMEMBER - SIMPLE SHAPES WORK BEST, AND ARE EASIER TO DRAW —

— HAVE A GO!

UNIFORM –

SWAG.

ALMOST EVERYONE SEEMS TO WEAR SOME KIND OF UNIFORM THESE DAYS, AND UNIFORM IS USEFUL IN A CARTOON BECAUSE YOU CAN SEE EXACTLY WHO EVERYONE IS!

WE EVEN USE UNIFORMS THAT DON'T REALLY EXIST –

– WELL, HAVE YOU EVER SEEN A BURGLAR IN A LONE RANGER MASK AND A STRIPED SHIRT?

YOU DON'T NEED A LOT OF DETAILS TO MAKE A UNIFORM EASY TO RECOGNISE –

– LOOK AT THE EXAMPLES ON THIS PAGE...

... NOW, TRY A FEW YOURSELF!

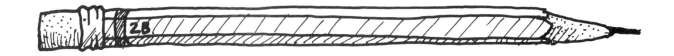

EVERY FACE TELLS A STORY...

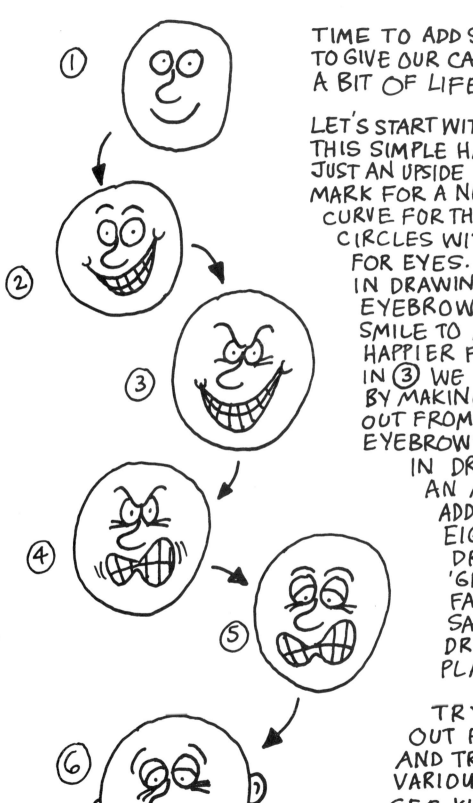

TIME TO ADD SOME FUNNY FACES TO GIVE OUR CARTOON CHARACTERS A BIT OF LIFE!

LET'S START WITH DRAWING ①. THIS SIMPLE HAPPY FACE IS JUST AN UPSIDE DOWN QUESTION MARK FOR A NOSE - A SIMPLE CURVE FOR THE MOUTH AND CIRCLES WITH DOTS IN THEM FOR EYES.
IN DRAWING ② WE ADD EYEBROWS AND A TOOTHY SMILE TO MAKE IT AN EVEN HAPPIER FACE.
IN ③ WE MAKE A SLY FACE BY MAKING THE EYES LOOK OUT FROM DOWN-POINTING EYEBROWS.
IN DRAWING ④ WE MAKE AN ANGRY FACE BY ADDING A 'FIGURE OF EIGHT' MOUTH.
DRAWING ⑤ IS A 'GRIN AND BEAR IT' FACE BY ADDING SAD EYES.
DRAWING ⑥ IS JUST PLAIN SAD!

TRY THESE FACES OUT FOR YOURSELF AND TRY MIXING THE VARIOUS FEATURES TO SEE WHAT YOU GET!

SURPRISED...

BORED...

RUDE...

PUZZLED...

* HERE ARE A FEW MORE EXAMPLES TO ADD TO YOUR COLLECTION...

PRACTISE THESE FACES — YOU WILL NEED THEM!

I HAVE DRAWN SOME 'BLANK' FACES BELOW FOR YOU TO COPY AND PRACTISE ON.

YOU CAN MAKE YOUR BASIC FACE INTO A MALE OR FEMALE FACE QUITE EASILY — JUST ADD THE RIGHT DETAILS...

YOU CAN HAVE FUN WITH ACCESSORIES TOO — SPECTACLES, BEARDS, EARRINGS,

ETC. ETC.

REMEMBER THAT IN CARTOONING YOU CAN DO ANYTHING THAT YOU WANT!

NOW WE COME TO THOSE ESSENTIAL EXTREMITIES...

WE'VE DRAWN STICK FIGURES...

WIGGLE" "WIGGLE"

WE'VE DRAWN FUNNY FACES...

WE'VE COVERED YOUNG AND OLD...

WE'VE EVEN BEEN DEDICATED FOLLOWERS OF FASHION...

AND NOW →

YOU NEED HANDS . . .

DRAWING HANDS IS EASY — START BY DRAWING A BUNCH OF BANANAS ①

ADD A THUMB AND SMOOTH THE BANANAS A LITTLE. THE STALK BECOMES THE CUFF. ②

YOU CAN MAKE YOUR HANDS MORE DETAILED IF YOU WANT TO BY ADDING FINGERNAILS AND WRINKLES. ③

I USUALLY DRAW HANDS WITH 3 FINGERS...

...HANDS CAN BE ROUNDED OR ANGULAR, BIG OR SMALL.

*USE YOUR OWN HANDS TO CHECK YOU GET THE THUMBS IN THE RIGHT PLACE.

AND FEET...

YOU CAN DRAW BARE FEET OR SHOES IN YOUR CARTOON.

START OUT WITH SOME SIMPLE SHAPES LIKE THE ONES BELOW.

HIGH HEELS - FLAT SOLES - PLATFORMS - THE LIST IS ALMOST ENDLESS!

DOES ANYONE REMEMBER WINKLE PICKERS?

YOU COULD EVEN HAVE TALKING SHOES IF YOU WANT TO...

19

LET'S START BY GIVING OUR CARTOON CREATIONS SOME ACCESSORIES –

– OR THINGS TO PLAY WITH...

NEWSPAPERS AND MAGAZINES TO READ,
MOBILE TELEPHONES TO ANNOY PEOPLE WITH,
LAPTOP COMPUTERS TO DRIVE THEM CRAZY,
ATTACHE CASES TO KEEP
SANDWICHES IN ...

...YOU CAN ADD CAMERAS AND VIDEOS TO THIS LIST,
ALONG WITH GARDENING TOOLS, COMPUTERS, FISHING
RODS, GOLF CLUBS, AND ANYTHING ELSE YOU FANCY.

PICK YOUR OWN FAVOURITE SUBJECT AND **TRY IT**!

NOW LET'S ADD SOME WORDS...

TIME TO GIVE OUR CARTOON CHARACTERS SOMEWHERE TO
WORK, REST AND PLAY!

COLLECT A SCRAPBOOK OF PHOTOGRAPHS OF A VARIETY OF LOCATIONS TO SET YOUR CARTOON ADVENTURES.

PUBS, SHOPS, SUPERMARKETS, SCHOOLS, LIBRARIES, CARS, RESTAURANTS, COLLEGES, OFFICE, BEACH, RAILWAY STATIONS, POLICE STATIONS, HOTELS, MOUNTAIN TOP, DESERT ISLANDS, NURSERY, HOSPITALS, ETC.

YOU CAN TRACE ROUND THESE PHOTOGRAPHS OR SKETCH REAL PLACES TO MAKE YOUR BACKGROUNDS.

DRAW YOUR CARTOON FIGURES IN A THICKER PEN THAN THE BACKGROUND TO HELP THEM STAND OUT.

DON'T PUT TOO MUCH DETAIL IN THE BACKGROUND OR YOUR CARTOON PEOPLE WILL DISAPPEAR UNDER A MASS OF LINES, TONES, AND TEXTURES!

CARICATURE

THIS CHEERFUL BLIGHTER IS ME!

SOONER OR LATER YOU ARE BOUND TO WANT TO HAVE A TRY AT DRAWING CARICATURES - AND WHY NOT - IT'S GREAT FUN!

AN EASY WAY TO MAKE A START WITH CARICATURES IS TO USE PHOTOGRAPHS...

...TRACE A FAIRLY ACCURATE VERSION OF A PHOTOGRAPH...

...NOW YOU CAN USE THIS AS A BASIS FOR YOUR OWN EXAGGERATED DRAWING.

PICK OUT THE FEATURES THAT ARE MOST NOTICEABLE.

THE CARICATURE SHOULD STILL BE RECOGNISABLE AS THE PERSON YOU HAVE DRAWN.

BE PATIENT—EVEN PROFESSIONAL CARTOONISTS HAVE TO WORK HARD ON CARICATURES!

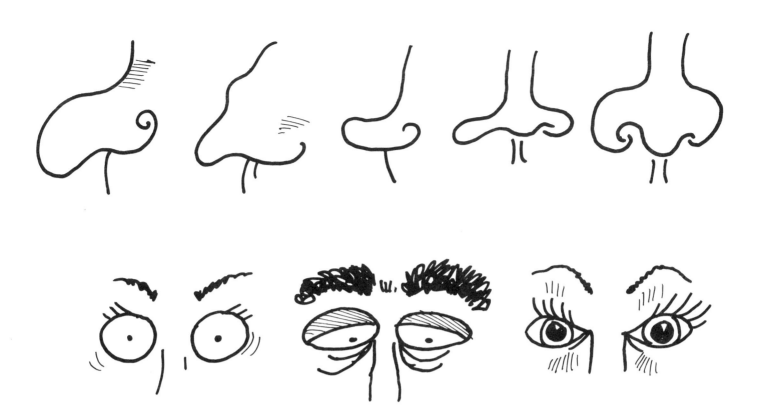

KEEP A SKETCHBOOK FULL OF DIFFERENT NOSES, EARS,
EYES AND MOUTHS TO USE IN YOUR CARICATURES.
YOU CAN USE THESE EXAMPLES - OR ALTER THEM FOR
YOUR OWN DRAWINGS...

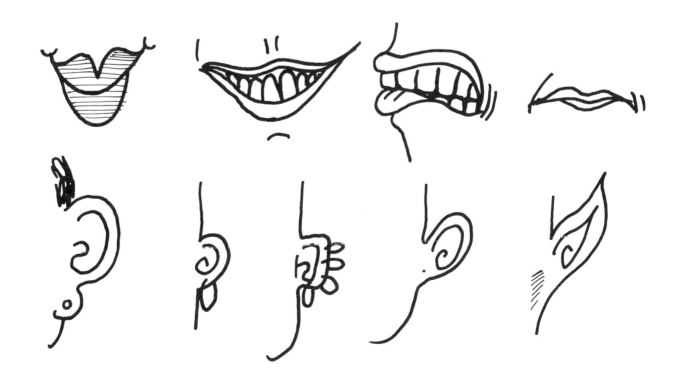

USE NEWSPAPER AND MAGAZINE PHOTOGRAPHS TO TRY CARICATURES OF THE RICH AND FAMOUS, OR EVEN INFAMOUS!

BEGIN AS BEFORE, WITH A FAIRLY ACCURATE TRACING···

···THEN EXAGGERATE THOSE FEATURES THAT MAKE YOUR CHARACTER RECOGNISABLE!

DON'T BE TOO CONCERNED IF NO ONE KNOWS WHO YOU'VE DRAWN – –JUST KEEP PRACTISING!

TRY NOT TO MAKE YOUR CARICATURES TOO EXAGGERATED OR UNPLEASANT...

..YOU MIGHT JUST UPSET SOMEONE YOU DON'T WANT TO!

I PREFER TO MAKE MY CARICATURES MORE "GLAMOROUS HOLLYWOOD" THAN "GORY HORROR MOVIE" — AND PEOPLE USUALLY ENJOY RECEIVING THEM AS PRESENTS

AND...

...ALWAYS SHOW THE CARICATURE TO THE PERSON YOU'VE DRAWN BEFORE YOU SHOW IT TO ANYONE ELSE —

—JUST TO BE ON THE SAFE SIDE!

29

STRIP CARTOONS GIVE YOU THE CHANCE TO TELL A STORY...

...EVEN IF IT IS AS OLD AS THIS ONE!

BELOW IS ONE OF THE FIRST STRIP CARTOONS I EVER HAD PUBLISHED — IT FOLLOWS THE SAME BASIC IDEA AS THE STRIP ABOVE. YOU CAN SEE IT TELLS A LITTLE STORY — EVEN IF YOU DON'T KNOW WHAT THE STORY IS ABOUT!

THIS STRIP WAS DRAWN FOR A **HAM RADIO** MAGAZINE.

* IF YOU HAVE UNUSUAL HOBBIES YOU MIGHT LIKE TO THINK UP SOME OF YOUR OWN STRIP IDEAS?!

I USUALLY WRITE MY STRIP CARTOON IDEAS OUT IN WORDS FIRST?

OUR LAST TRIANGLE PLAYER...

..DISAPPEARED...

..WHILE WE WERE PLAYING THE BERMUDA SYMPHONY!

THEN I DO A ROUGH LAYOUT USING STICK FIGURES?

OUR LAST TRIANGLE PLAYER...

..DISAPPEARED.!

WHILE WE WERE PLAYING THE BERMUDA SYMPHONY!

IF I'M HAPPY I DRAW THE WHOLE THING PROPERLY?

OUR LAST TRIANGLE PLAYER...

TALES FROM... THE PIT!

...DISAPPEARED...

..WHILE WE WERE PLAYING THE BERMUDA SYMPHONY!

HEE HEE

SOMETIMES I DRAW PICTURES FIRST — JUST FOR A CHANGE!

32

USE LOTS...

...OF DIFFERENT SIZE AND SHAPE "BOXES"...

...TO ADD VARIETY TO YOUR STRIP!

ALSO... USE LOTS OF DIFFERENT LETTERING...

LIKE ZAP and BOOM

and KKKKEEEERRRUUUNNCH!

and DRIP

...THEN...

USE PLENTY OF DIFFERENT IMAGES IN YOUR STRIP CARTOON BOXES — TRY EXTREME CLOSE-UPS, CRAZY ANGLES OF VIEW OR SILHOUETTES...

SHOW THE PASSAGE OF TIME ✳

NEVER BE AFRAID TO TRY SOMETHING NEW ~ WHO KNOWS WHERE IT WILL LEAD?!

MAKE SURE...

THAT THE SPACES YOU LEAVE FOR THE WORDS TO FIT INTO..

ARE THE RIGHT SIZE!

YOU CAN DRAW STRIP CARTOONS ABOUT ANYTHING — WORK, HOBBIES, POLITICS, SPORT, MUSIC ~ YOU NAME IT!

MORRIS'S GARAGE...

CONNON'S CARS

SO—THIS IS THE ACTUAL M.G...

...THAT ONCE BELONGED TO JACK CLOG..

THE INTERNATIONALLY FAMOUS CLOWN—KNOWN FOR HIS ...

EXPERIMENTS WITH EJECTOR SEATS!

WHOOSH

I HATE IT WHEN HE'S DEPRESSED...

...IT'S ALWAYS MY T.V. AERIAL HE SITS ON!

PETER COULE ©'85

LANCE

AH! SALTPOT SALTPOT SHINING BRIGHT.. ON MY TABLE DAY AND NIGHT..

... WHEN ALL AT ONCE I SAW A CROWD... A HOST OF GOLDEN BREAKFAST GRILLS!

THIS CREATIVE WRITING COURSE HAS CERTAINLY IMPROVED HIS LANGUAGE...

RABBIT RABBIT RABBIT...

WHAT THE &#!

...EXCEPT WHEN THE RETECTION SLIPS ARRIVE!

KEEP YOUR IDEAS NICE AND SIMPLE TO BEGIN WITH.

GO ON ~ TRY ONE!

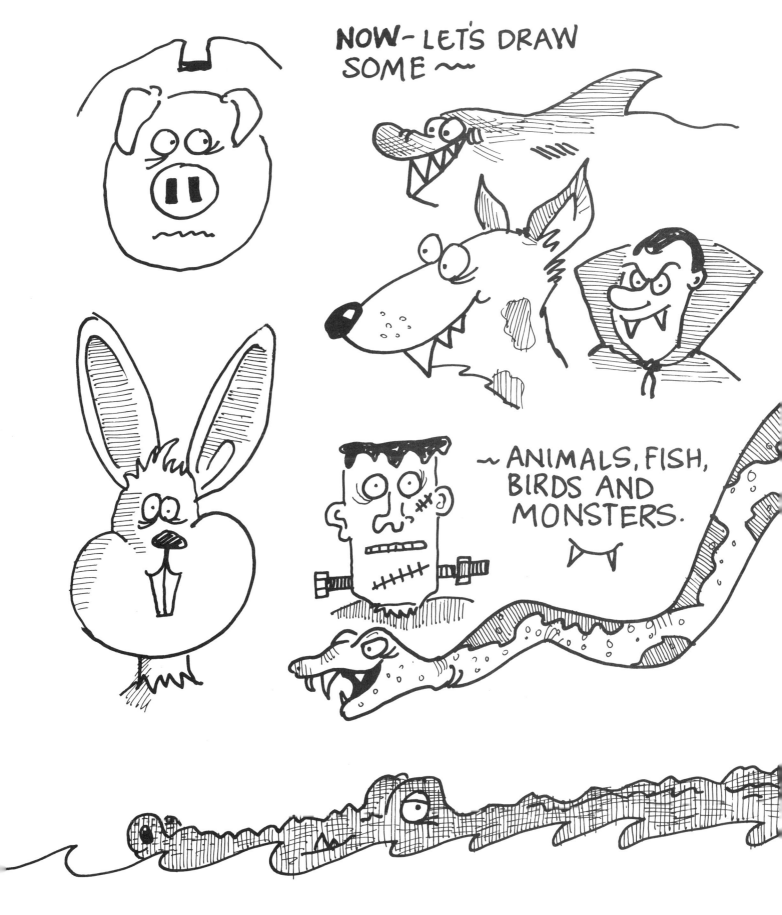

NOW—LET'S DRAW SOME ~~~

~ ANIMALS, FISH, BIRDS AND MONSTERS.

WE WILL ALSO COVER TALKING TEAPOTS, VICIOUS VACUUM CLEANERS AND INEBRIATE INSECTS!

TO DRAW ANIMALS START WITH THE SIMPLE FACE SHOWN ON THE RIGHT...

A CAT IS JUST A TRIANGLE WITH A TAIL AND A FLUFFY ROUND FACE ON TOP!

DRAW THIS SIMPLE FACE

THIS FACE IS VERY ADAPTABLE

I HAVE USED IT FOR A DOG AND A HAMSTER AS WELL

PRACTISE DRAWING THIS BASIC FACE AND SEE WHAT YOU CAN DO WITH IT!

CARTOON ANIMALS CAN ALSO IMITATE PEOPLE — BY ADDING HUMAN DRESS AND MANNERISMS...

...THIS IS CALLED 'ANTHROPOMORPHISM'.

YOU CAN GIVE ANIMALS JOBS OR HOBBIES THAT SUIT THEIR ANIMAL INSTINCTS!

A HOUND DOG SHOULD MAKE A GREAT DETECTIVE. WITH HIS LONG FLOWING MANE THE LION ALREADY LOOKS LIKE A SOCCER STAR!

*
REMEMBER TO INCLUDE MALE AND FEMALE — YOUNG AND OLD.

TO KEEP THE LION ON THE PREVIOUS PAGE COMPANY WE HAD BETTER DRAW SOME MORE JUNGLE ANIMALS.
THE GIRAFFE HAS A TRIANGULAR HEAD, THE MONKEY'S FACE IS HEART SHAPED. A CROCODILE'S MOUTH IS A 'V' SHAPE FULL OF TEETH! THE HIPPO IS VERY SIMPLE TO DRAW ~ LOTS OF BLOBS, SMALL EARS AND STUMPY TEETH.
TRY SOME...

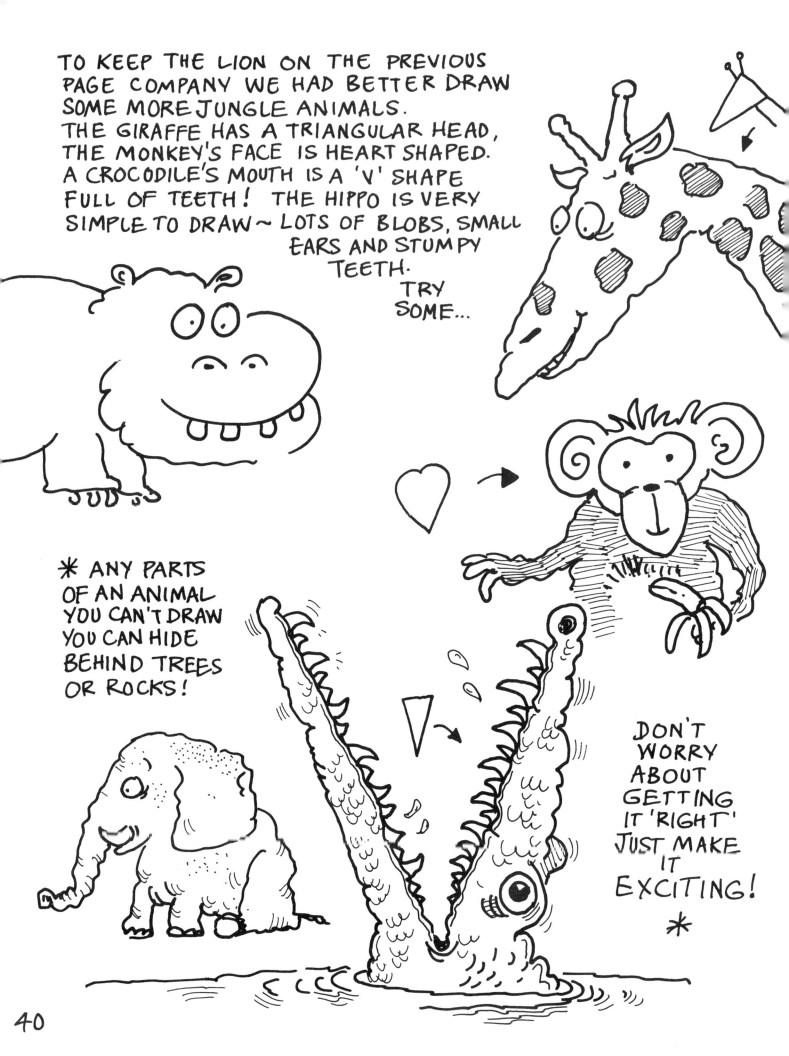

* ANY PARTS OF AN ANIMAL YOU CAN'T DRAW YOU CAN HIDE BEHIND TREES OR ROCKS!

DON'T WORRY ABOUT GETTING IT 'RIGHT' JUST MAKE IT EXCITING!
*

40

TWO HEART SHAPES GIVE YOU THE BASIC SHAPE OF THE OWL — YOU CAN ALSO DRAW BIRDS THAT EXIST ONLY IN YOUR OWN IMAGINATION!

THE SIMPLE BLOB SHAPES USED TO CONSTRUCT THE TWO DUCKS BELOW — ALLOW YOU TO DRAW THEM IN OR OUT OF THE WATER — JUST ADD FEET!

BASIC SHAPE

* YOU CAN MAKE A BIRD ANY SHAPE YOU FANCY — AS LONG AS IT HAS A BEAK!

AN EASY WAY TO DRAW FEATHERS — WRITE THE LETTER W OVER AND OVER AGAIN...

* REMEMBER...

TO GIVE YOUR 'CREATURE CREATIONS' A FULL RANGE OF EXPRESSIONS...

MAKE THEM HAPPY, SAD, ANGRY, PUZZLED, SURPRISED...

* PRACTISE THE SIMPLE FACE.

YOU CAN DISPENSE WITH PEOPLE ALTOGETHER IF YOU WANT TO!

TRY A STRIP CARTOON * WITH A CAST OF ANIMALS INSTEAD OF HUMANS!

MENU

42

FISH CAN ALSO APPEAR IN OUR CARTOONS- WITH A VARIETY FROM THE EVER HUNGRY SHARK TO THE BIG 'SOFTIE' OF THE SEA - THE WHALE.

USE THE SIMPLE SHAPE I HAVE DRAWN BELOW TO GET YOU STARTED...

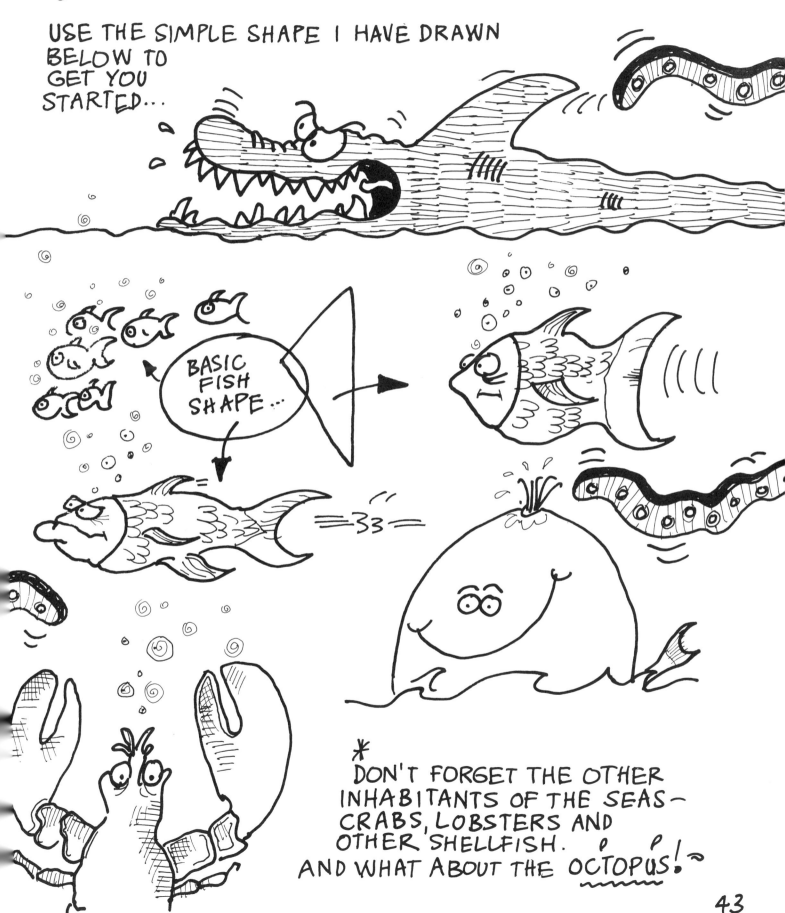

BASIC FISH SHAPE...

* DON'T FORGET THE OTHER INHABITANTS OF THE SEAS - CRABS, LOBSTERS AND OTHER SHELLFISH. AND WHAT ABOUT THE OCTOPUS!

IF YOU FANCY A BIT OF TIME-TRAVEL WHY NOT ADD A FEW
DINOSAURS...

START WITH A
SIMPLE 'BLOB'
SHAPE — THEN ADD
A LONG NECK
AND TAIL — AS
LONG AS YOU
LIKE ...
LOTS OF
SHARP
FANGS
COMPLETE
THE PICTURE.

ADD
LOTS OF
SCALES
TO THE
BACKS.

COMBINE
YOUR DINOSAURS
WITH SOME SIMPLE
CAVEMEN (+ WOMEN)
AND YOU WILL HAVE
THE BASIS FOR
SOME GREAT ACTION
CARTOONS!

MONSTERS COME IN ALL SHAPES AND SIZES — FROM THE TRADITIONAL FIERY DRAGON TO A SHAPELESS BLOB

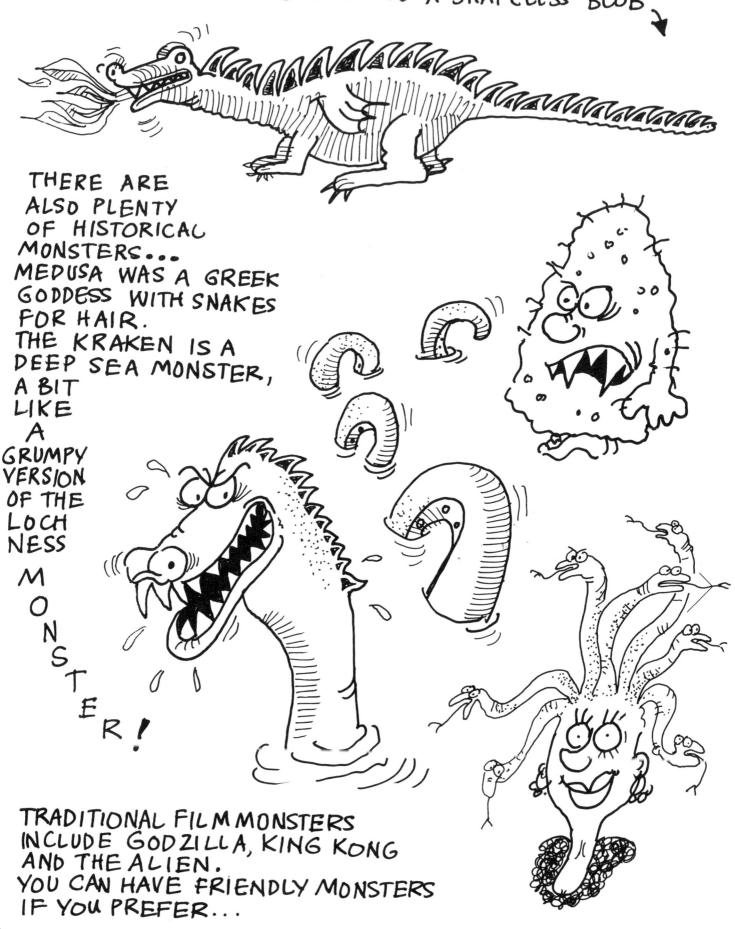

THERE ARE ALSO PLENTY OF HISTORICAL MONSTERS...
MEDUSA WAS A GREEK GODDESS WITH SNAKES FOR HAIR.
THE KRAKEN IS A DEEP SEA MONSTER, A BIT LIKE A GRUMPY VERSION OF THE LOCH NESS MONSTER!

TRADITIONAL FILM MONSTERS INCLUDE GODZILLA, KING KONG AND THE ALIEN.
YOU CAN HAVE FRIENDLY MONSTERS IF YOU PREFER...

SPEAKING OF ALIENS—
REMEMBER THAT
OUTER SPACE IS JUST
A PEN OR PENCIL
STROKE AWAY...

... SPACE ALIENS CAN
BE FUNNY OR
FRIGHTENING—AND
ANY SIZE OR SHAPE
THAT YOU FANCY!

REMEMBER TO PUT THEM
ONTO CRAGGY PLANETS
WITH LOTS OF
CRATERS.

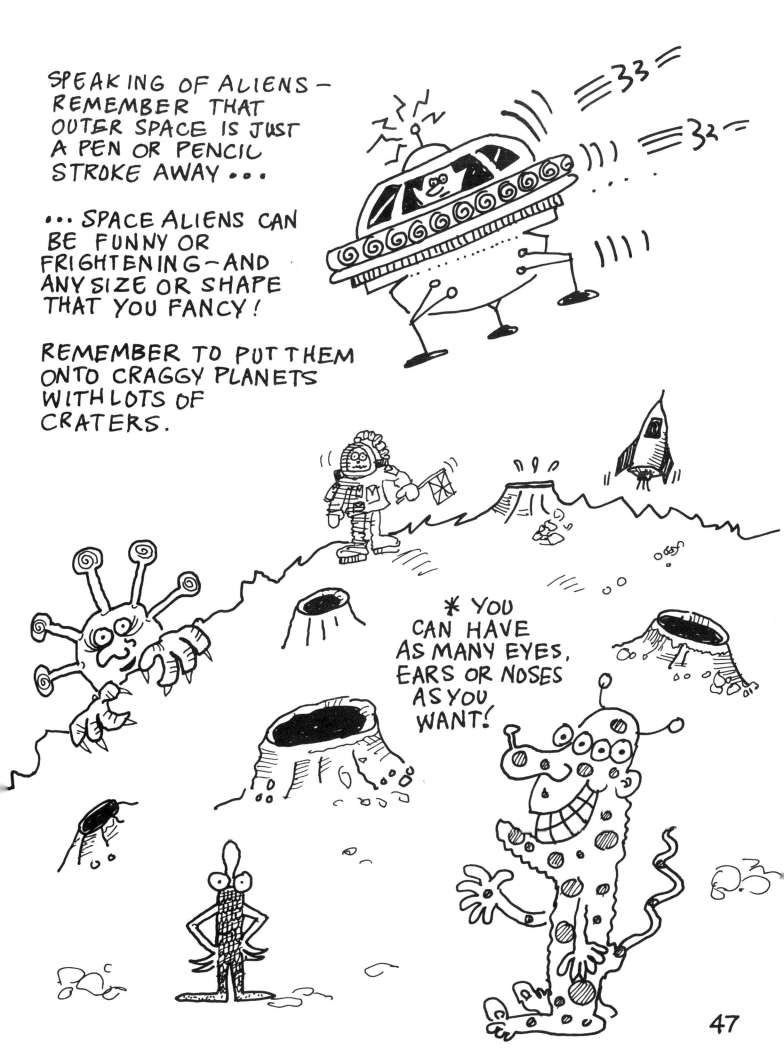

* YOU
CAN HAVE
AS MANY EYES,
EARS OR NOSES
AS YOU
WANT!

FRANKENSTEIN, WOLFMAN AND DRACULA ARE SOME OTHER TRADITIONAL MONSTERS YOU MIGHT LIKE TO HAVE A GO AT DRAWING.

PLENTY OF STITCHES TO SHOW THAT HE IS MADE UP OF SPARE PARTS

SHINY HAIR

STARING, BLOODSHOT EYES

FANGS

BLACK CAPE

A SIMPLE GHOST IS JUST A FLOATING SHAPE WITH EYES...

CHANGING ROOM

YOU COULD HAVE YOUR OWN GHOSTLY COMIC OR CARTOON STRIP.

YOU CAN ALSO BRING OTHER THINGS TO LIFE — PENS AND PENCILS, COMPUTERS, TEAPOTS, GOLF CLUBS, EVEN TALKING SHOES!

START WITH A SIMPLE SKETCH OF THE OBJECT YOU WANT TO BRING TO LIFE — THEN ADD EXPRESSIONS AND GESTURES TO SUIT THE CHARACTER.

HB

REMEMBER TO USE SIMPLE SHAPES ☐ △ ◯ ⬭ TO HELP YOU BUILD THE CARTOON.

ANIMATION

MAKE YOUR CARTOONS MOVE!

TO MAKE THE SORT OF ANIMATED CARTOON YOU SEE ON T.V. OR AT THE CINEMA, A SERIES OF IMAGES - EACH ONE SLIGHTLY DIFFERENT - ARE PROJECTED QUICKLY ON TO A SCREEN. AS THE BRAIN CAN'T KEEP UP WITH THE EVER CHANGING IMAGES IT SIMPLY LETS THEM FLOW TOGETHER— GIVING THE IMPRESSION OF MOVEMENT!

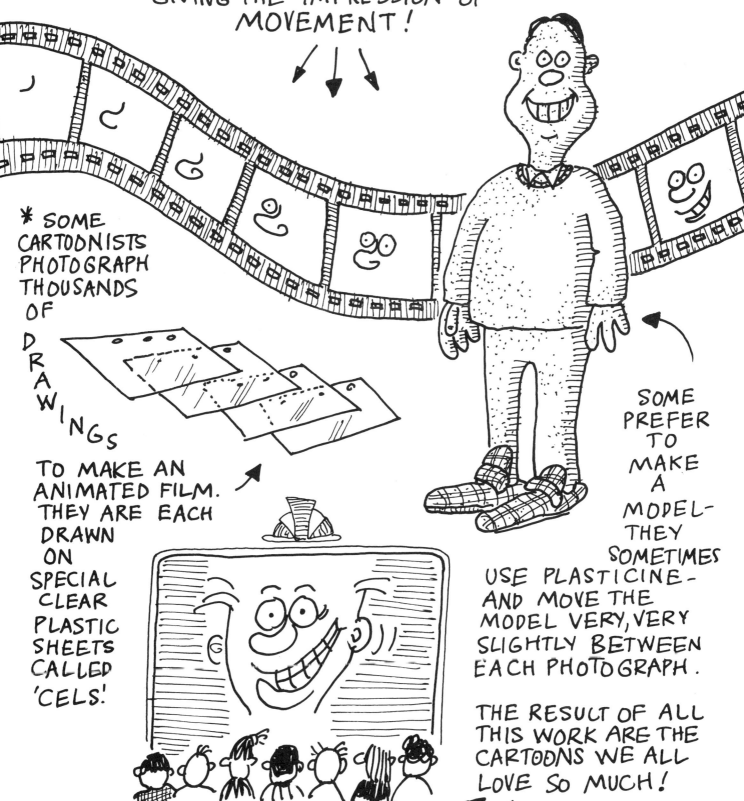

* SOME CARTOONISTS PHOTOGRAPH THOUSANDS OF DRAWINGS TO MAKE AN ANIMATED FILM. THEY ARE EACH DRAWN ON SPECIAL CLEAR PLASTIC SHEETS CALLED 'CELS'!

SOME PREFER TO MAKE A MODEL- THEY SOMETIMES USE PLASTICINE - AND MOVE THE MODEL VERY, VERY SLIGHTLY BETWEEN EACH PHOTOGRAPH.

THE RESULT OF ALL THIS WORK ARE THE CARTOONS WE ALL LOVE SO MUCH!

51

TRY MAKING A "FLICKER" BOOK... DRAW A SIMPLE FACE ON THE LAST PAGE OF A SKETCHBOOK. ON THE PREVIOUS PAGE DRAW A SLIGHTLY DIFFERENT FACE

* YOU CAN USE ANY SIMPLE MOVEMENTS IN A "FLICKER" BOOK — FROM FUNNY FACES TO BOUNCING BALLS! TRY SOME!

.. GO BACK ANOTHER PAGE AND ADD ANOTHER FACE. WHEN YOU HAVE DRAWN 20 to 30 FACES, FLICK THE PAGES .....➤

* TRY DRAWING A FACE — ONE FEATURE AT A TIME — OR CHANGE THE EXPRESSION ON A FACE...

IT'S GOOD DRAWING PRACTISE TOO!

PENCIL FLIPS...

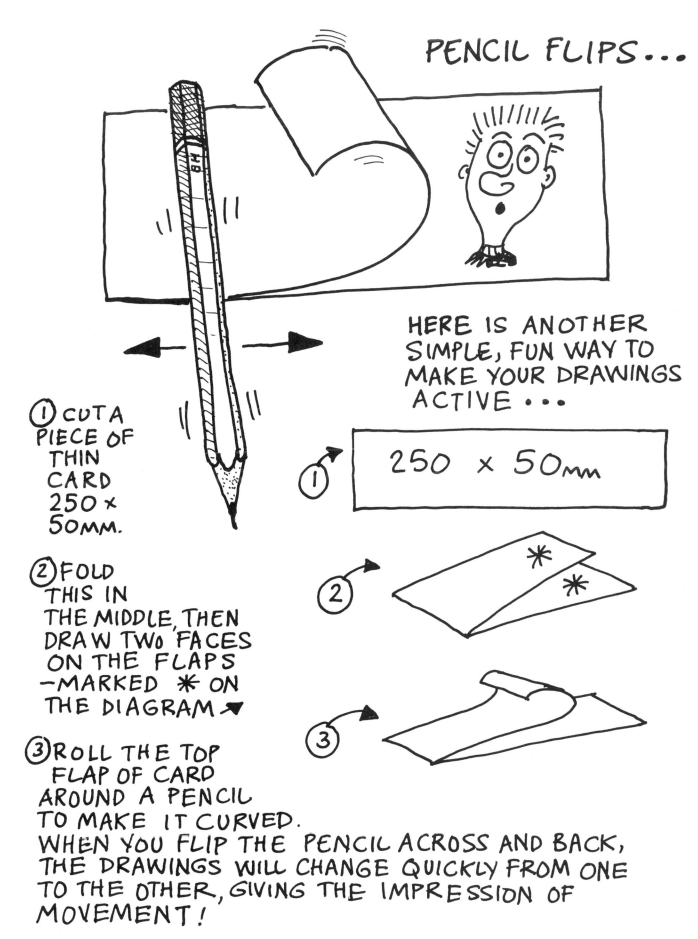

HERE IS ANOTHER SIMPLE, FUN WAY TO MAKE YOUR DRAWINGS ACTIVE...

① CUT A PIECE OF THIN CARD 250 × 50mm.

① 250 × 50mm

② FOLD THIS IN THE MIDDLE, THEN DRAW TWO FACES ON THE FLAPS —MARKED ✳ ON THE DIAGRAM ↗

②

③ ROLL THE TOP FLAP OF CARD AROUND A PENCIL TO MAKE IT CURVED. WHEN YOU FLIP THE PENCIL ACROSS AND BACK, THE DRAWINGS WILL CHANGE QUICKLY FROM ONE TO THE OTHER, GIVING THE IMPRESSION OF MOVEMENT!

③

✳ TRY DRAWING FIREWORKS EXPLODING, HUMPTY DUMPTY FALLING OFF HIS WALL OR QUICK CHANGING EXPRESSIONS!

SPINNERS ARE EASY TO MAKE...
JUST CUT OUT TWO CIRCLES AND DRAW YOUR TWO
DIFFERENT IMAGES ON THEM. NOW TAPE THEM
EITHER SIDE OF A PEN OR
PENCIL AND TWIST BETWEEN
YOUR FINGERS TO SEE
THE ACTION!

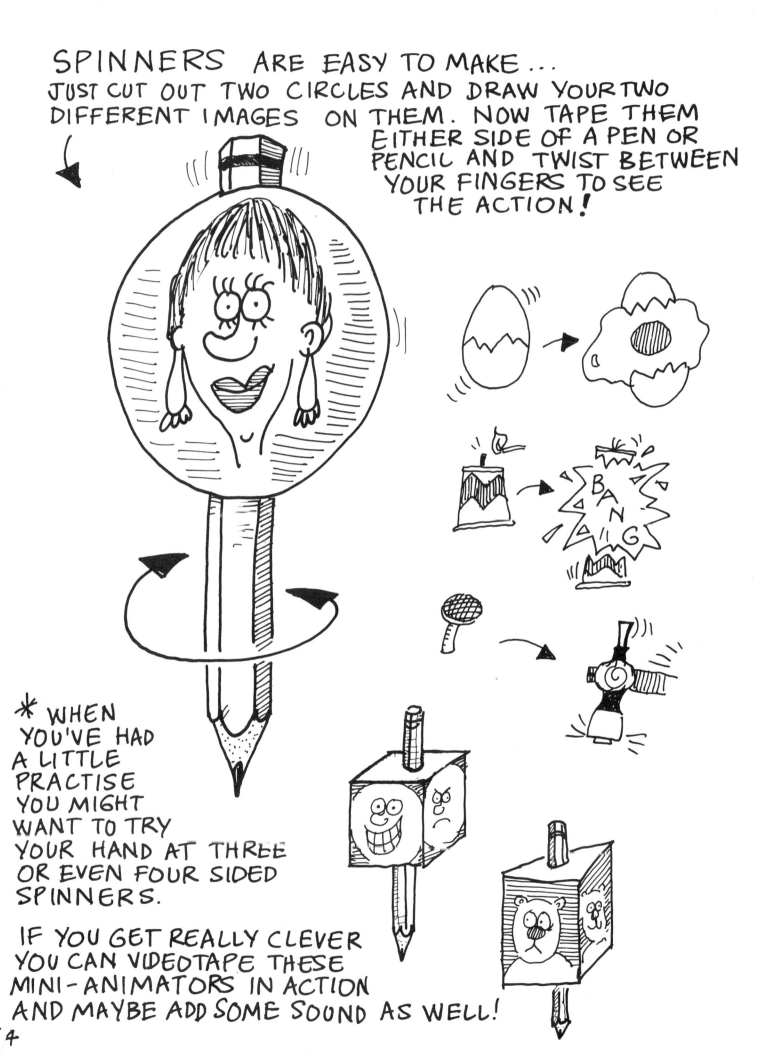

* WHEN
YOU'VE HAD
A LITTLE
PRACTISE
YOU MIGHT
WANT TO TRY
YOUR HAND AT THREE
OR EVEN FOUR SIDED
SPINNERS.

IF YOU GET REALLY CLEVER
YOU CAN VIDEOTAPE THESE
MINI-ANIMATORS IN ACTION
AND MAYBE ADD SOME SOUND AS WELL!

NOW ALL YOU NEED TO DRAW YOUR VERY OWN ORIGINAL CARTOONS ARE SOME JOKE IDEAS...

...DON'T WORRY

EMPTY!

HELP

IS AT HAND!

THINKING UP YOUR OWN IDEAS FOR CARTOONS IS NOT AS DIFFICULT AS YOU MIGHT THINK. OVER THE NEXT FEW PAGES I WILL SHOW YOU SOME OF THE METHODS THAT I USE TO GET MY CREATIVE JUICES FLOWING...

TRY MY METHODS FIRST AND SEE HOW YOU GET ON - THEN TRY AND THINK UP SOME JOKE CREATING IDEAS FOR YOURSELF.

SOMETIMES WORKING WITH A FRIEND CAN HELP - THERE IS OFTEN SOMEONE YOU KNOW WHO SEEMS TO HAVE AN ENDLESS SUPPLY OF JOKES AND STORIES!

CONTRASTS

LARGE AND SMALL – NEAT AND SCRUFFY –
GENEROUS AND MEAN – STRONG AND WEAK –
WET AND DRY – FAST AND SLOW – LONG AND SHORT –
HELPFUL AND DIFFICULT – BOXER AND BALLET DANCER...

THESE ARE ALL CONTRASTS – OPPOSITES IF YOU PREFER.

LET'S TAKE ONE – STARTING WITH THE BOXER –

NOW WE'LL MIX IN THE OPPOSITE OR CONTRAST IDEA –
IN THIS CASE A BALLET DANCER...

HERE'S ONE IDEA –
LET'S SEE WHAT YOU COME UP WITH

* TRY AND SPOT CONTRASTS
IN THE WORK OF YOUR OWN
FAVOURITE CARTOONISTS.

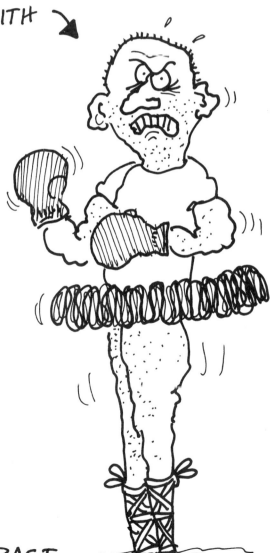

REALLY, WHICH ONE?!

I'VE JUST HAD A HAIR CUT.

56

THIS IS A NEAT/SCRUFFY CONTRAST.

VISUAL CARTOONS

VISUAL CARTOONS RELY ON PICTURES TO MAKE YOU LAUGH RATHER THAN WORDS. SOMETIMES VISUAL CARTOONS HAVE SIGNS IN THEM, LIKE THESE...

... KEEP OFF THE GRASS
... NO SMOKING
... DANGER
... WE SERVE SNAILS
... OPEN ALL HOURS

SOMETIMES ALL YOU NEED IS A SINGLE WORD TO SET YOU OFF

KEEP OFF THE GRASS

THE CARTOON ABOVE WAS INSPIRED BY THE WORD **TRIPOD!**

58

YOU DON'T NEED ANY WORDS TO TELL YOU THAT THESE "ANGELS" ARE IN A HURRY!

THE ESKIMO CARTOON CAME FROM A HOT/COLD CONTRAST IDEA.

PROP CARTOONS....

... HAPPEN WHEN YOUR CARTOON CHARACTERS DO ODD OR BIZARRE THINGS WITH "EVERYDAY OBJECTS", OR WHEN THESE THINGS TAKE ON A LIFE OF THEIR OWN — LIKE TALKING COMPUTERS!
THINK OF NEW USES FOR A VARIETY OF EVERYDAY THINGS LIKE SWEEPING BRUSHES —

BLOGGS
BRUSHES
STAFF GAMES ROOM

* START OUT BY SKETCHING A FEW ITEMS CONNECTED WITH YOUR FAVOURITE TOPIC— MAYBE PHOTOGRAPHY

SEE WHAT YOUR CARTOON CHARACTERS CAN DO WITH...

...TELEPHONES
FRYING PANS
SWEEPING BRUSHES
T.V. REMOTES
STAPLERS
CRASH HELMETS
CAMERAS

ETC. ETC. ETC.

NOW **DRAW** THEM!

58

SURPRISE ENDING CARTOONS...

ARE LIKE A 'JACK-IN-THE-BOX' - THE JOKE SHOULD SPRING OUT WHEN YOU LEAST EXPECT IT!

* KEEP THE "PUNCH LINE" UNTIL THE LAST POSSIBLE MOMENT!

SURPRISE ENDINGS WORK WELL IN COMICS AND STRIP CARTOONS.

HERE ARE A FEW EXAMPLES FOR YOU TO PLAY WITH -

① MY CAR HAS ENGINE TROUBLE - IT BROKE DOWN ON A LEVEL CROSSING AND GOT HIT BY THE ENGINE!

② I THINK YOU SHOULD MARRY FOR LOVE - AND I'M GOING TO FALL IN LOVE WITH THE FIRST MILLIONAIRE I MEET.

③ I WAS A BIT WORRIED WHEN I SAW A FISH IN THE PIANO - THEN I REALISED IT WAS A PIANO TUNA!

④ I FINALLY STOPPED THE RABBITS FROM DIGGING UP MY GARDEN - I HID ALL THE SPADES!

IF ALL ELSE FAILS TO PROMPT AN IDEA, THEN YOU CAN ALWAYS FALL BACK ON THE

CLICHÉ.

THESE ARE CARTOON SITUATIONS THAT SEEM TO PRODUCE AN ENDLESS STREAM OF JOKE IDEAS —

WHY NOT TRY THEM ?

PRIVATE KEEP OFF

* DESERT ISLANDS
WAITING ROOMS
ALIEN LANDINGS
LAUNDERETTES
OFFICES — SHOPS
CLASSROOMS
PUBS AND CLUBS
ABOMINABLE SNOWMEN
PRISONS — WEDDINGS
TRAFFIC JAMS, ETC ...

I WOULD HAVE BEEN HERE SOONER BUT I COULDN'T FIND A PARKING SPACE!

BY NOW YOU SHOULD BE BUILDING UP QUITE A NUMBER OF CARTOONS AND CARTOON IDEAS. OVER THE NEXT FEW PAGES I WILL SHOW YOU SOME OF THE THINGS YOU CAN DO WITH ALL THE STUFF YOU PRODUCE...

YOU CAN FRAME YOUR BEST CARTOON IDEAS, AND HANG THEM IN YOUR HOME OR GIVE THEM AS PRESENTS.

* YOU CAN BUY SIMPLE, INEXPENSIVE PICTURE FRAMES FROM PHOTO. SHOPS AND DEPARTMENT STORES.

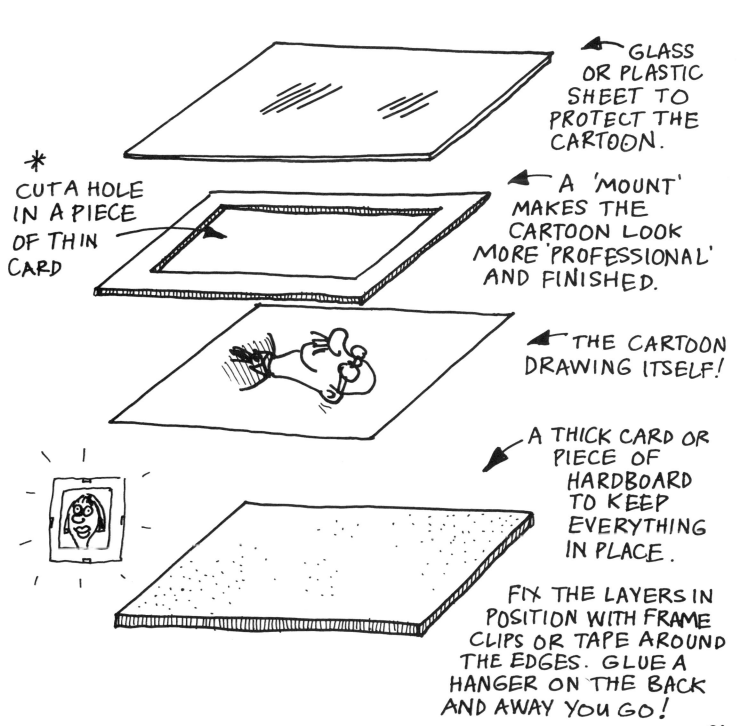

GLASS OR PLASTIC SHEET TO PROTECT THE CARTOON.

* CUT A HOLE IN A PIECE OF THIN CARD

A 'MOUNT' MAKES THE CARTOON LOOK MORE 'PROFESSIONAL' AND FINISHED.

THE CARTOON DRAWING ITSELF!

A THICK CARD OR PIECE OF HARDBOARD TO KEEP EVERYTHING IN PLACE.

FIX THE LAYERS IN POSITION WITH FRAME CLIPS OR TAPE AROUND THE EDGES. GLUE A HANGER ON THE BACK AND AWAY YOU GO!

CARDS FOR BIRTHDAYS, CHRISTMAS, EASTER, ETC. ARE ALWAYS WELCOME — AND EVEN MORE SO IF YOU HAVE MADE THEM YOURSELF!

A4 PAPER

* DRAW YOUR DESIGN AS SHOWN ~ THEN FOLD ALONG THE DOTTED LINES

IF YOU WANT A LARGER QUANTITY, HAVE THE DRAWING PHOTOCOPIED.

FINISHED CARD.

A4 PAPER

* IN THIS CARD ↗ WE FOLD THE PAPER TO MAKE A LONG, THIN DESIGN. THIS GIVES 3 'PAGES' FOR THE JOKE OR MESSAGE … HERE IS AN EXAMPLE —

① → ROSES ARE RED… ② → VIOLETS ARE BLUE… ③ → I HOPE YOU LOVE ME, 'COS I LOVE YOU!

WHILE WE ARE ON THE SUBJECT OF CARDS - WHY NOT HAVE A TRY AT THIS MONSTER POP-UP CARD!

COPY THE IMAGE I'VE DRAWN HERE OR DRAW YOUR OWN

DRAW A MONSTER FACE, FOLD DOWN THE DOTTED LINE AND GLUE THE "BOLTS" ONTO A SHEET OF A4 PAPER, FOLDED DOWN THE MIDDLE.

* ADD PLENTY OF SCARS AND STITCHES TO MAKE A TRULY HORRIBLE FACE!

TRY WOLFMAN MUMMY DRACULA AND MORE...

WHEN YOU CLOSE THE CARD THE FACE FOLDS NEATLY UP INSIDE ~ AND SPRINGS OUT WHEN THE CARD IS OPENED!

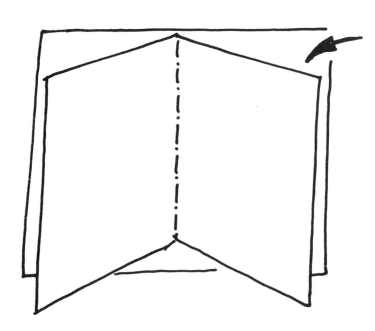

A SHEET OF FAIRLY STIFF A4 PAPER, FOLDED IN THE MIDDLE.

THE FACE FOLDS FORWARD - THE CARD FOLDS BACK.

WHY NOT MAKE A SIMPLE
PUPPET!
DRAW AND CUT OUT A HEAD AND BODY SHAPE. ADD ARMS, HANDS, LEGS AND FEET. FIX STRINGS TO HEAD AND ELBOWS AND YOU'VE GOT IT!
FIX THE PARTS TOGETHER WITH PAPER FASTENERS (BUY THESE FROM A STATIONERY SHOP).

CUT THE SHAPES FROM STIFF CARD AND YOUR PUPPET WILL LAST QUITE A LONG TIME.

MAKE A FEW OF YOUR FAMILY, FRIENDS OR "FAVE" POP STARS OR FOOTBALLERS!

YOU CAN MAKE THEM AS LARGE OR AS SMALL AS YOU LIKE. LIFE SIZE IF YOU CAN FIND ENOUGH CARD AND BIG ENOUGH FASTENERS!

MAKE HOLES HERE FOR JOINING.

A GREAT WAY OF SHOWING OFF YOUR CARTOONS IS TO PUT THEM ONTO...

KITES!

THERE ARE LOTS OF DIFFERENT KITE SHAPES - THE ONE SHOWN HERE IS A "DIAMOND".

* IF YOU DON'T FANCY MAKING A KITE - BUY A WHITE ONE AND COLOUR IT WITH FABRIC PAINTS!

① CUT 2 STICKS - 75 CM AND 55.CM - FASTEN INTO A CROSS 19CM FROM THE TOP OF THE LONGER STICK. TIE STRING ALL ROUND THE EDGE OF THE CROSS. ② GLUE A PAPER COVERING ON THE FINISHED DIAMOND SHAPE. ③

FIX A 1 METRE LENGTH OF STRING FROM TOP TO BOTTOM STICKS AND MAKE A LOOP 20CM ABOVE THE JOINT OF THE CROSS - TIE YOUR FLYING LINE TO THIS LOOP AND ENJOY!

* FLY SAFELY - AWAY FROM OVERHEAD OBSTRUCTIONS AND NEVER IN THE RAIN!

MAKE A LONG TAIL FROM PAPER BOWS, TO KEEP THE KITE STABLE. ABOUT 5 METRES WILL DO!

ADD THE DESIGN OF YOUR CHOICE

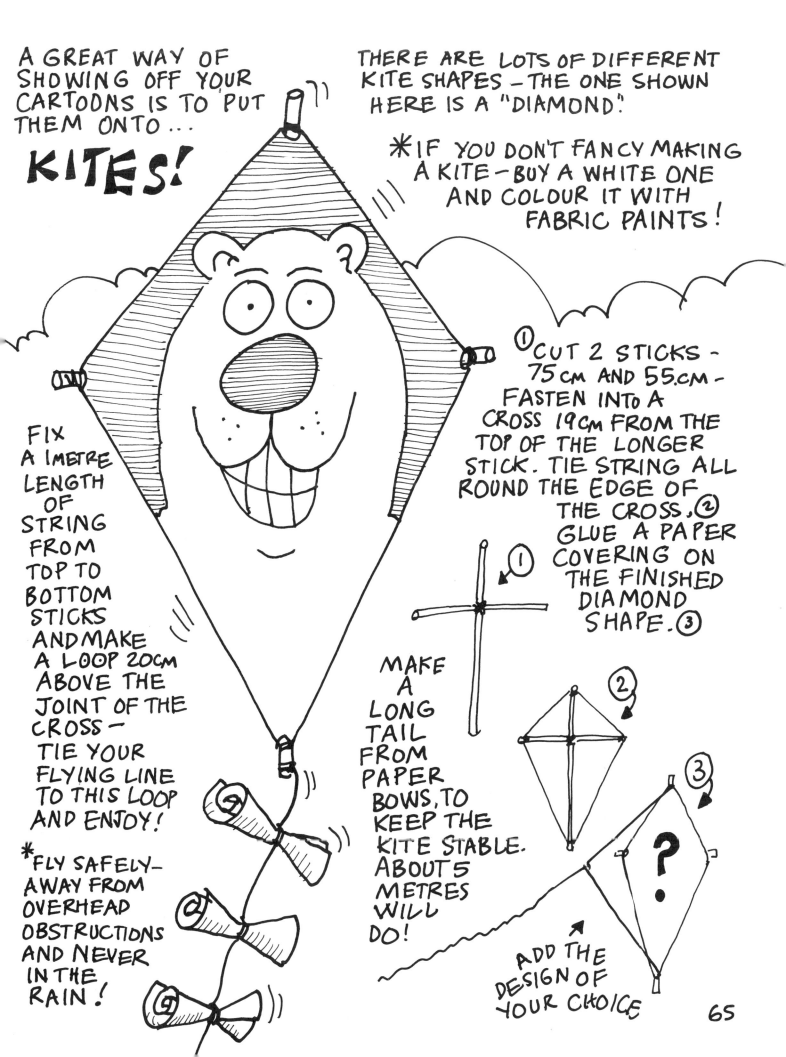

65

IF YOU CAN GET HOLD OF SOME MODELLING MATERIAL WHY NOT MAKE YOUR VERY OWN...

PENCIL TOPPERS...

STICK A BLOB OF MODELLING MATERIAL

ON THE END OF A PENCIL AND MODEL A FACE...

..ADD SMALLER BLOBS FOR EARS, NOSE AND MOUTH.

✳ WHEN YOUR PENCIL TOPPER IS DRY YOU CAN PAINT IT WITH ACRYLIC COLOURS.

?
WHY NOT TRY A SELF-PORTRAIT ?

✳ WHEN YOUR PENCIL RUNS OUT JUST PULL THE TOPPER OFF AND PUT IT ON A NEW ONE!

MAKE YOUR NEXT PARTY IRRESISTIBLE BY DESIGNING YOUR OWN PERSONALISED CARTOON INVITATIONS!

DRAW THE DESIGN ON THIN CARD — REMEMBER ALL THE ESSENTIAL INFORMATION — AND HAVE COPIES MADE TO SEND OUT TO FRIENDS OR FAMILY.

COME TO A PARTY ... SATURDAY JULY 20th ... 8 TILL LATE. JIM + SAL.

BARBECUE PARTY

PARTY INVITATIONS.

TO MAKE THEM EVEN MORE INTERESTING YOU CAN CUT THE SHAPE OUT OF THE CARD →

THESE COULD BECOME COLLECTORS ITEMS!

STEVE'S 18th BIRTHDAY 8 TO 11·30

SATURDAY MAY 6th

BRING A CAN

BIRTHDAY CARDS CAN BE DONE AS A CARICATURE FOR A SPECIAL PERSON!

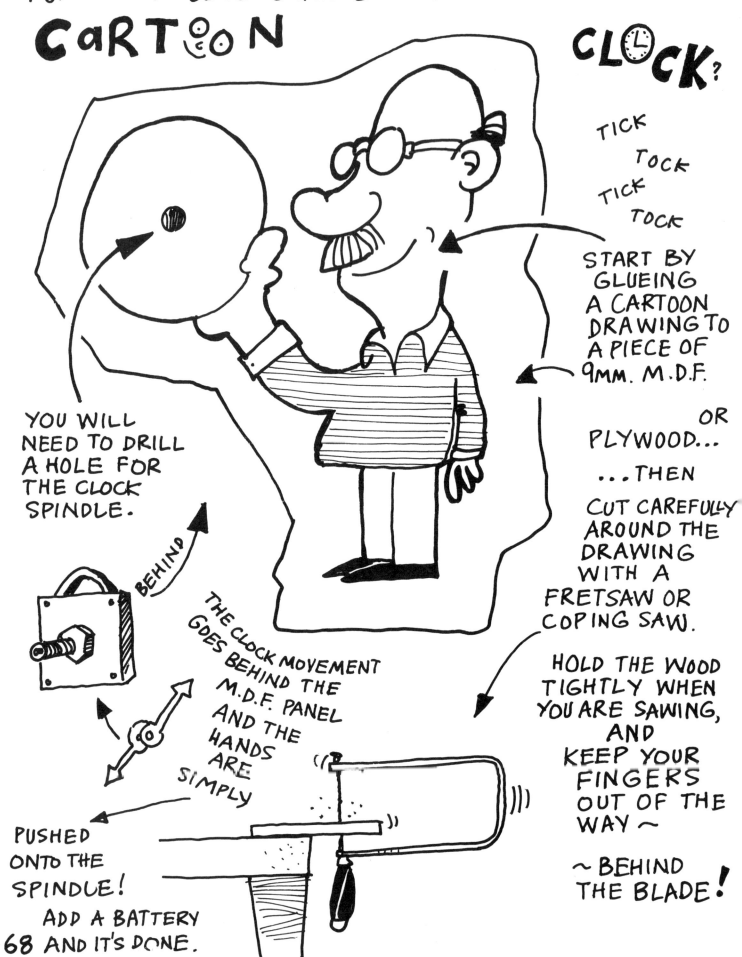

FOR A COMPLETE CHANGE - WHY NOT MAKE A
CARTOON

CLOCK?

TICK

TOCK

TICK

TOCK

START BY GLUEING A CARTOON DRAWING TO A PIECE OF 9MM. M.D.F.

OR PLYWOOD...

...THEN

CUT CAREFULLY AROUND THE DRAWING WITH A FRETSAW OR COPING SAW.

HOLD THE WOOD TIGHTLY WHEN YOU ARE SAWING, AND KEEP YOUR FINGERS OUT OF THE WAY ~

~ BEHIND THE BLADE!

YOU WILL NEED TO DRILL A HOLE FOR THE CLOCK SPINDLE.

BEHIND

THE CLOCK MOVEMENT GOES BEHIND THE M.D.F. PANEL AND THE HANDS ARE SIMPLY

PUSHED ONTO THE SPINDLE!

ADD A BATTERY AND IT'S DONE.

68

FOR THE **ULTIMATE** IN SELF-ADVERTISING THERE IS NOTHING BETTER THAN YOUR VERY OWN, ORIGINAL ...

... 👕 SHIRT !

* YOU CAN EITHER DRAW THE CARTOON DIRECTLY ONTO THE 'T' SHIRT WITH FABRIC DYES OR PAINTS <u>OR</u> →

BEER BELLY ?

<u>NOTE</u> – SOME FABRIC DYES NEED IRONING TO FIX THEM – DO THIS CAREFULLY AND **SAFELY !**

→ SOME PRINTERS WILL PUT YOUR CARTOON ONTO A 'T' SHIRT USING A PHOTOGRAPHIC PROCESS.

DO ONE FOR **EVERYBODY !**

WHY NOT MAKE A
MOBILE
FROM ALL YOUR CARTOONS?

THE CARTOONS CAN BE ANY SIZE OR SHAPE, AND THE HANGING FRAME CAN BE ANY SIZE!

PASTE YOUR SPARE CARTOONS ON THIN CARD AND HANG FROM THE CEILING.

USE * DOWEL, CANE OR WIRE

* GLUE OR TIE THE STICKS TOGETHER TO MAKE THE HANGING FRAME.

I'M SURE THAT YOU WILL THINK UP EVEN MORE WAYS TO DISPLAY YOUR CARTOONING TALENTS ONCE YOU GET STARTED...

OVER THE NEXT FEW PAGES WE WILL LEARN SOME

ADVANCED DRAWING TECHNIQUES!

TO MAKE YOUR
CARTOONS EVEN
BETTER —

— DON'T WORRY THEY ARE **EASY**!

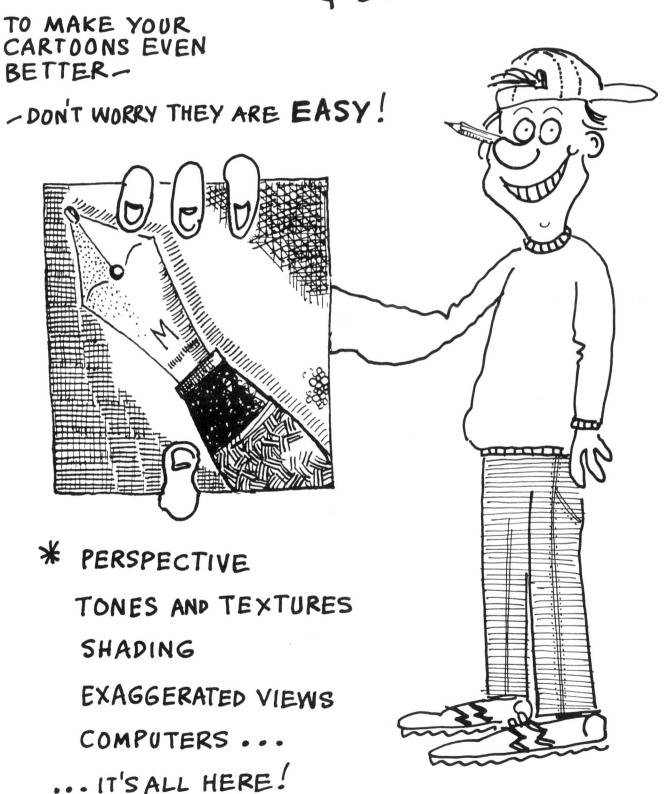

* PERSPECTIVE

TONES AND TEXTURES

SHADING

EXAGGERATED VIEWS

COMPUTERS ...

... IT'S ALL HERE!

SHADOWS MAKE OBJECTS LOOK MORE "SOLID" AND THREE DIMENSIONAL...

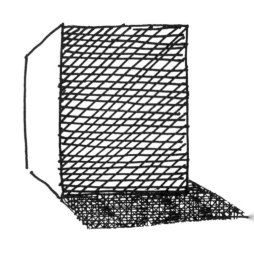

...SIMPLY PLACE THE SHADOW ON THE OPPOSITE SIDE TO THE LIGHT SOURCE.

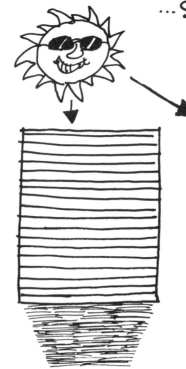

WITHOUT SHADOWS THIS 'BOX' IS JUST A COLLECTION OF LINES!

* 'NORMAL' LIGHTING FOR A PERSON COMES FROM ABOVE.. (SUN OR CEILING LIGHTS)

SHADOW

TONES AND TEXTURES ALSO HELP TO MAKE THINGS LOOK MORE SOLID BY SHOWING WHAT THEY ARE MADE FROM. THERE ARE A FEW EXAMPLES BELOW ~ AND I HAVE USED MANY OTHERS THROUGHOUT THIS BOOK.

SHADING CAN BE NEAT AND PRECISE OR "SCRIBBLY" — DRAW IN THE STYLE THAT YOU FEEL MOST COMFORTABLE WITH!

* PRACTISE AND USE THESE IDEAS.

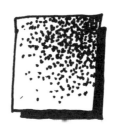

PERSPECTIVE SIMPLY MEANS THAT AS THINGS GET FURTHER AWAY FROM YOU THEY APPEAR SMALLER - LOGICAL ENOUGH!

— IN THE SIMPLE DRAWING OF A BEDSIDE CABINET BELOW I HAVE EXAGGERATED THIS EFFECT TO SHOW HOW IT WORKS. THE TOP AND FRONT GET SMALLER THE FURTHER AWAY THEY ARE...

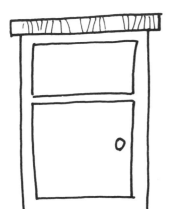

START A PERSPECTIVE DRAWING WITH A TRIANGLE SHAPE — AS THINGS GET NEARER THE POINT OF THE TRIANGLE THEY GET SMALLER — EVENTUALLY THEY VANISH!
THIS IS CALLED THE VANISHING POINT!

IT'S TRUE!

IN THE DRAWING BELOW, THE NEARER JOGGER IS BIGGER THAN THE ONE BEHIND. I HAVE ALSO DRAWN HIM WITH A THICKER PEN TO MAKE HIM STAND OUT EVEN MORE.

* OF COURSE IF YOU FIND THE WHOLE THING TOO DULL — THEN SIMPLY IGNORE IT ALL AND DRAW THE WAY YOU ENJOY!

PERSPECTIVE IS VERY USEFUL IF YOU WANT TO EXPERIMENT WITH STRANGE ANGLES OF VIEW... LIKE··'WORM'S EYE AND 'BIRD'S VIEW' EYE VIEW'

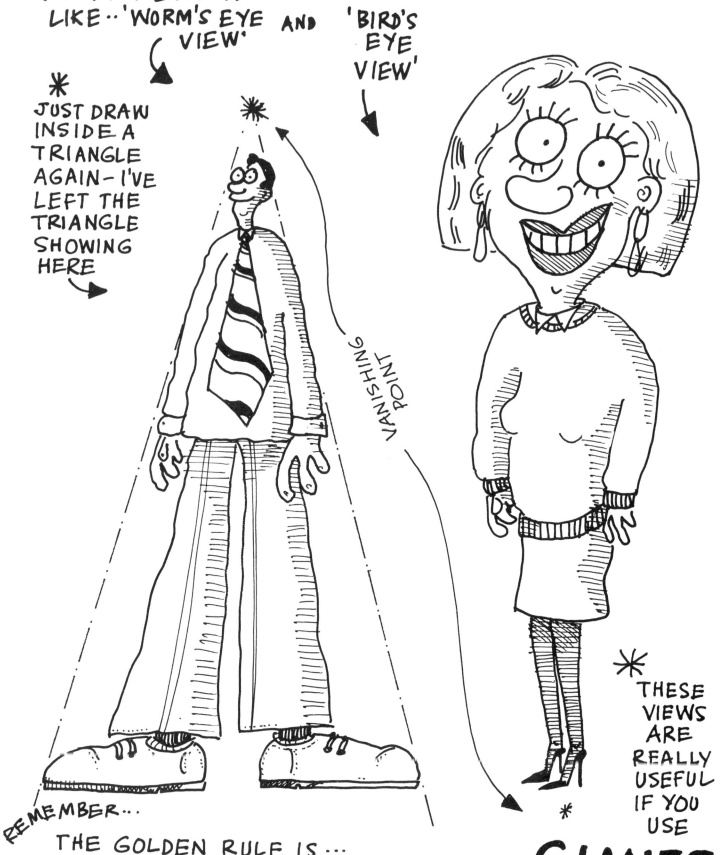

* JUST DRAW INSIDE A TRIANGLE AGAIN - I'VE LEFT THE TRIANGLE SHOWING HERE

VANISHING POINT

* THESE VIEWS ARE REALLY USEFUL IF YOU USE

REMEMBER...

THE GOLDEN RULE IS ... THINGS NEARER TO YOU ARE

BIGGER!

GIANTS IN YOUR CARTOONS!

IF YOU ARE FORTUNATE ENOUGH TO HAVE ACCESS TO A COMPUTER YOU CAN PRODUCE YOUR CARTOONS ON THIS.
A SIMPLE DRAWING OR PAINTING PACKAGE WILL ENABLE YOU TO CREATE AN ENDLESS NUMBER OF CHARACTERS AND SITUATIONS.
YOU CAN CREATE A 'DATABASE' OF DIFFERENT EARS, EYES, NOSES, MOUTHS, FACES, ETC. ETC AND COMBINE THESE IN ENDLESS POSSIBILITIES...

YOU MIGHT EVEN BE ABLE TO PRINT YOUR CARTOONS.

SOME COMPUTERS ALSO RUN ANIMATION SOFTWARE — SO YOU CAN EVEN PRODUCE YOUR OWN ANIMATED CARTOONS!

LIGHTS - CAMERA - ACTION...

75

TECHNICAL STUFF...

PUZZLED BY PENS?

BOTHERED BY BRUSHES?

PERPLEXED BY PAPER SIZES?

* WORRY NO MORE! OVER THE NEXT FEW PAGES I WILL EXPLAIN ALL THE ESSENTIAL INFORMATION YOU NEED TO KNOW TO CONVERSE IN FLUENT "CARTOONSPEAK"

PAPER, PENS AND PENCILS...

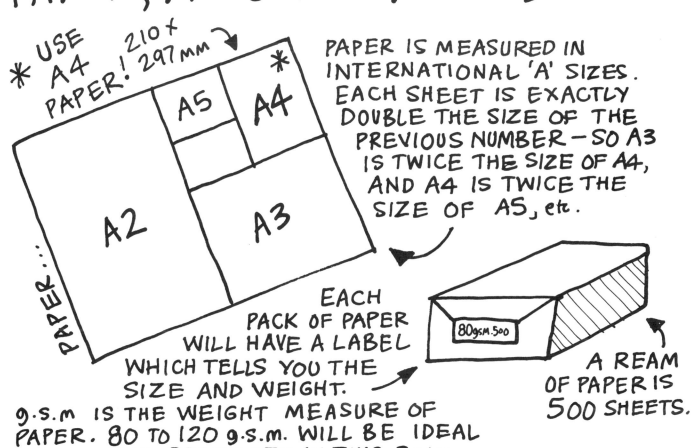

* USE A4 PAPER! 210 x 297mm

PAPER IS MEASURED IN INTERNATIONAL 'A' SIZES. EACH SHEET IS EXACTLY DOUBLE THE SIZE OF THE PREVIOUS NUMBER — SO A3 IS TWICE THE SIZE OF A4, AND A4 IS TWICE THE SIZE OF A5, etc.

PAPER...

A5 A4
A2 A3

EACH PACK OF PAPER WILL HAVE A LABEL WHICH TELLS YOU THE SIZE AND WEIGHT.

80gsm.500

A REAM OF PAPER IS 500 SHEETS.

g.s.m IS THE WEIGHT MEASURE OF PAPER. 80 TO 120 g.s.m. WILL BE IDEAL FOR ALL THE PROJECTS IN THIS BOOK.

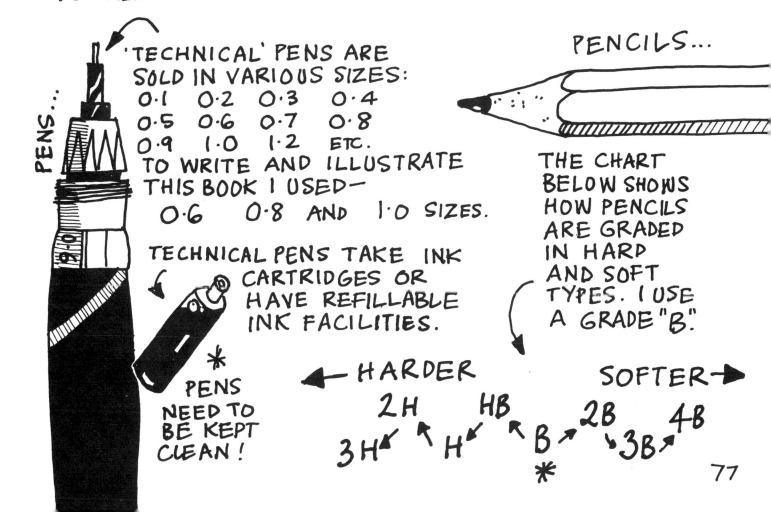

PENS...

'TECHNICAL' PENS ARE SOLD IN VARIOUS SIZES:
0·1 0·2 0·3 0·4
0·5 0·6 0·7 0·8
0·9 1·0 1·2 ETC.
TO WRITE AND ILLUSTRATE THIS BOOK I USED —
0·6   0·8 AND 1·0 SIZES.

TECHNICAL PENS TAKE INK CARTRIDGES OR HAVE REFILLABLE INK FACILITIES.

* PENS NEED TO BE KEPT CLEAN!

PENCILS...

THE CHART BELOW SHOWS HOW PENCILS ARE GRADED IN HARD AND SOFT TYPES. I USE A GRADE "B."

← HARDER
2H   HB
3H ↗ ↑ H ↗ ↘ B ↗ 2B 4B
                        3B
SOFTER →
*

USE INDIAN INK IN "DIP" PENS, AND WASH THE NIB AFTERWARDS – DON'T USE THIS INK IN FOUNTAIN PENS AS IT WILL CLOG THEM UP! TYPING CORRECTION FLUID WILL COVER UP YOUR MISTAKES AND A SOFT PLASTIC ERASER WILL REMOVE PENCIL LINES WITHOUT SCRATCHING THE PAPER

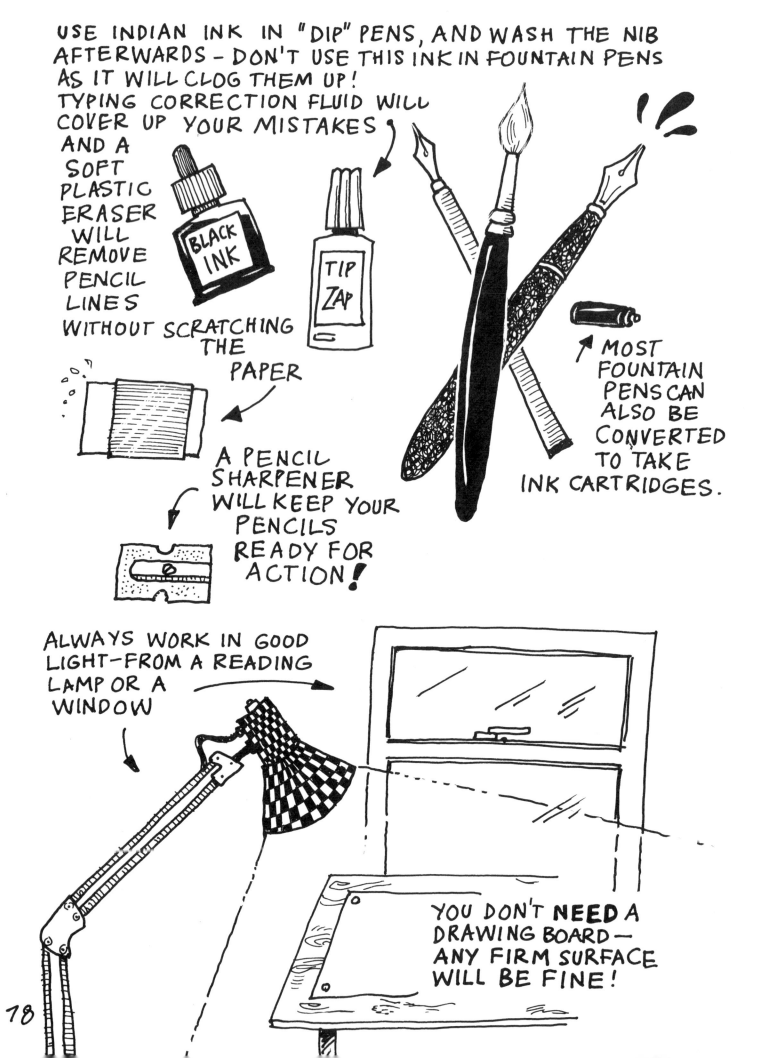

BLACK INK

TIP ZAP

A PENCIL SHARPENER WILL KEEP YOUR PENCILS READY FOR ACTION!

MOST FOUNTAIN PENS CAN ALSO BE CONVERTED TO TAKE INK CARTRIDGES.

ALWAYS WORK IN GOOD LIGHT – FROM A READING LAMP OR A WINDOW

YOU DON'T **NEED** A DRAWING BOARD – ANY FIRM SURFACE WILL BE FINE!

PAPER, PENS AND PENCILS...

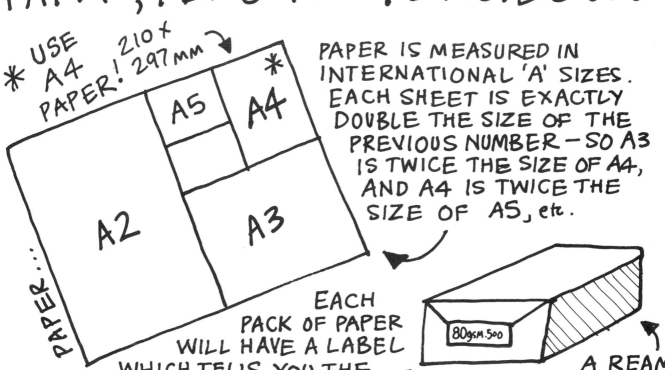

* USE A4 PAPER! 210 x 297 MM

A5 A4
A2
A3

PAPER...

PAPER IS MEASURED IN INTERNATIONAL 'A' SIZES. EACH SHEET IS EXACTLY DOUBLE THE SIZE OF THE PREVIOUS NUMBER — SO A3 IS TWICE THE SIZE OF A4, AND A4 IS TWICE THE SIZE OF A5, etc.

EACH PACK OF PAPER WILL HAVE A LABEL WHICH TELLS YOU THE SIZE AND WEIGHT.

80gsm.500

A REAM OF PAPER IS 500 SHEETS.

g.s.m IS THE WEIGHT MEASURE OF PAPER. 80 TO 120 g.s.m. WILL BE IDEAL FOR ALL THE PROJECTS IN THIS BOOK.

PENS...

'TECHNICAL' PENS ARE SOLD IN VARIOUS SIZES:

0·1   0·2   0·3   0·4
0·5   0·6   0·7   0·8
0·9   1·0   1·2   ETC.

TO WRITE AND ILLUSTRATE THIS BOOK I USED —

0·6   0·8   AND   1·0 SIZES.

TECHNICAL PENS TAKE INK CARTRIDGES OR HAVE REFILLABLE INK FACILITIES.

* PENS NEED TO BE KEPT CLEAN!

PENCILS...

THE CHART BELOW SHOWS HOW PENCILS ARE GRADED IN HARD AND SOFT TYPES. I USE A GRADE "B."

← HARDER

SOFTER →

3H   2H   H   HB   B   2B   3B   4B

*

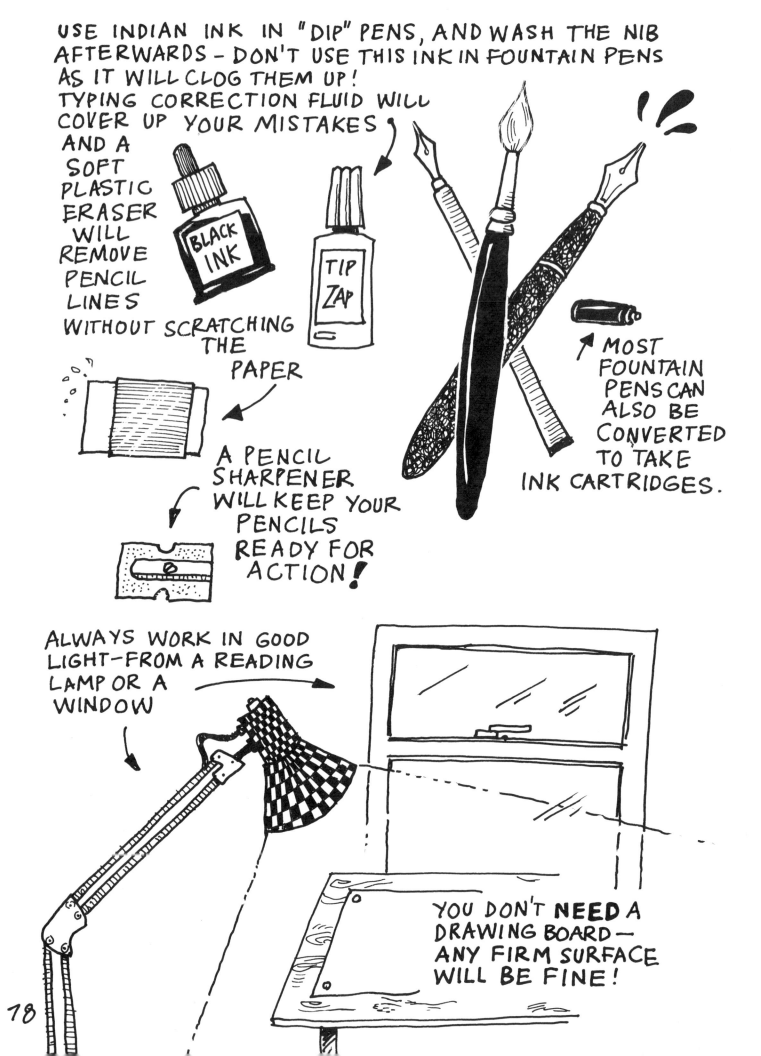

USE INDIAN INK IN "DIP" PENS, AND WASH THE NIB AFTERWARDS - DON'T USE THIS INK IN FOUNTAIN PENS AS IT WILL CLOG THEM UP! TYPING CORRECTION FLUID WILL COVER UP YOUR MISTAKES AND A SOFT PLASTIC ERASER WILL REMOVE PENCIL LINES WITHOUT SCRATCHING THE PAPER

BLACK INK

TIP ZAP

MOST FOUNTAIN PENS CAN ALSO BE CONVERTED TO TAKE INK CARTRIDGES.

A PENCIL SHARPENER WILL KEEP YOUR PENCILS READY FOR ACTION!

ALWAYS WORK IN GOOD LIGHT - FROM A READING LAMP OR A WINDOW

YOU DON'T **NEED** A DRAWING BOARD - ANY FIRM SURFACE WILL BE FINE!

78

* WELL—
THAT'S
ABOUT
ALL
YOU
NEED
TO
KNOW
TO
MAKE
A FLYING START AS A
CARTOONIST!

START WITH
SIMPLE STICK
FIGURES—
THEN
LEARN
TO
DRAW
FACES
?

PRACTISE
YOUR
CARICATURES?

LATER...
AND... COMICS + STRIPS

AND
INCLUDE SOME OF
THESE IN CARTOON
STRIPS AND COMICS~

DON'T FORGET TO ADD
ANIMALS AND MONSTERS
TO ADD VARIETY....

YOU
CAN
ALSO
PLAY AROUND WITH ANIMATION,
THINK UP YOUR VERY OWN
JOKES
AND EVEN USE
YOUR NEW SKILLS
MAKING MODELS
AND CARDS!

AND
PRACTISE
YOUR
DRAWING
TECHNIQUES—
WHAT ARE YOU WAITING FOR?

Well...

• ... I HOPE THAT "ANYONE CAN BE A CARTOONIST" HAS INSPIRED YOU TO TAKE UP THIS FASCINATING ART FOR YOURSELF.

* YOU WILL BE AMAZED AT JUST HOW QUICKLY YOUR SKILLS WILL DEVELOP WITH REGULAR PRACTISE —AND IF YOU ALREADY HAVE A PEN AND PENCIL CLOSE BY WHY NOT MAKE A START RIGHT **NOW!**

REMEMBER— YOU DON'T NEED ANY SPECIAL SKILLS OR QUALIFICATIONS TO DRAW CARTOONS ~

~ JUST THE DESIRE TO **HAVE A GO!**

GOOD LUCK —